D0866563

2

uman

The Essays

First published in Italy
in 2010 by
Skira Editore S.p.A.
Palazzo Casati Stampa
via Torino 61
20123 Milano
Italy
www.skira.net

Printed and bound in Italy.
First edition

ISBN: 978-88-572-0723-0

Distributed in North America
by Rizzoli International Publications,
Inc., 300 Park Avenue South,
New York, NY 10010, USA.
Distributed elsewhere in the world
by Thames and Hudson Ltd.,
181A High Holborn, London WC1V 7QX,
United Kingdom.

Sir Roy Strong

majorelle

men's fashion and garden fashion

SKIRA

U

The photographer and designer, **Sir Cecil Beaton**, was the most elegant gardener that I have ever known. As a young man I used to stay with him in the country at Reddish House, Broadchalke in Wiltshire.

There he created a garden which he prized, one with sweeping lawns, herbaceous borders, roses swagged on ropes, masses of lavender and all sorts of old-fashioned flowers framed by the deep green of clipped yew.

He indeed was the first person to take me around a garden he had made himself and hence was a seminal influence on my own garden-making. **But he had an elegance about everything he did, including a supreme elegance of appearance.** Not for him donning old worn-out clothes to go into the garden, an attitude typified by another great gardener I knew, Valerie Finnis,

Lady Scott, whose greatest accolade was to bestow on a visitor a coat which stood up in its own mud in which to tour the garden!

In contrast Cecil assumed a nonchalant informality with boots into which he tucked his trousers, an open-necked shirt with a loosely tied cravat, a waistcoat or jacket and, above all, his signature sombrero or fedora. With a trug on his arm, in which nestled a pair of secateurs, he paced the garden snipping off the odd dead rose or gathering a bouquet of flowers for guests to take back to town.

In this way he indicated that although he was the garden's owner he was not averse to extending a hand and engaging a little in the practicalities. That, it must be said, is an English characteristic.

On the continent I have noticed that it is considered déclassé to indulge in any way in hands-on gardening, a sharp contrast to the roll-call of English aristocratic owners who do not hesitate to garden and do not in the least feel that by doing so they lose status.
But then gardening in England is seen as a shared passion at once crossing and uniting the whole spectrum of society.

It was not always so. Placed within the perspective of the history of fashion, clothes for the garden fall into two distinct categories, those which, in English terms, we would designate as for gentlemen as against those for players. There is the dress of those who labour and that of those for whom they labour. The two do not really fuse until the second half of the twentieth century when the soaring cost of gardeners rendered most garden-owners more often than not part of the labour force.

It is worthwhile looking at the attire of the working gardener, for so much in fashion has emerged from designers noticing work clothes and upgrading them into another world. One of the earliest records of gardeners at work is an engraving of Spring dated 1570 after Pieter Bruegel the Elder. Gardeners are busy digging, weeding, planting, raking, training, pruning and watering a geometric garden. They wear hats to protect their heads from the sun as much as from the rain. Some are skullcaps, others with a brim. On their feet there are tough leather shoes with soles strong enough to push a spade into the earth.

They wear stockings, trunk hose and shirts with rolled-up sleeves along with jackets or waistcoats. **One striking feature is the apron into which a gardener could tuck small tools and lengths of twine or string.**

Almost seventy years on, in 1628, Jacques Callot produced two charming engravings of gardeners, one of them grafting a tree and the other contemplating a lily. The silhouette has changed to one which echoes that of the cavalier period but what is noticeable is that the distinctive elements remain the same: a hat, in both cases broad-brimmed, and an apron into whose strings one of them has tucked a large pruning knife.

Moving on to the next century a canvas from a series of eight depicting one of the great gardens of eighteenth-century England, Hartwell House, Buckinghamshire, shows not only elegant company but gardeners about their work rolling greensward and paths, scything grass and placing the clippings into baskets. Once again we encounter knee breeches, shoes and stockings and shirts with the sleeves rolled up and jackets. And again the ubiquitous hat appears.

A final snapshot completes the story. **Nathaniel Lloyd was the creator of the legendary garden at Great Dixter in Kent and also the father of the great plantsman and garden guru, Christopher. His book 'Garden Craftsmanship in Yew and Box' published in 1929 contains a number of photographs of his gardeners.** By then trousers have replaced breeches and the hat is a trilby but the rolled-up shirt sleeves, waistcoat

and apron would not have been out of
place four centuries earlier. All of these
images give elements which, when worn,
speak of the garden, in particular the
hat and the apron or, rather what that
embodied, a capacious pocket into which
to place things.

I add to this gallery one irresistible
image, a mid-seventeenth-century
engraving entitled *Habit de Jardinier*.
Here is a figure leapt from the world
of Arcimboldo for his arms are flowerpots
and his torso a plant container while
the skirts of his jacket together with
his breeches and stockings consist
of festoons of fruit and flowers, while
his hat is an explosion of produce.
In one hand he clasps a watering can
while, in the other, he supports a bundle
of tools such as a rake and hoe.
I know of no other image of a working
gardener which is so utterly fantastic.

That weird aberration, however, carries within it a degree of truth for his clothes are a reflection of so many of the elements which compose a garden. **And it is a hint that, yes, there is a symbiotic relationship between garden style and fashion in dress. It is not there in the earliest stages of garden-making in Western Europe, for it is only in the fourteenth century that they emerge as prestige symbols for the royal and aristocratic classes.** There is, however, little connexion between the late medieval hortus conclusus, a walled enclosure with turf seats and raised beds full of plants like irises, lilies, violets and pinks along with miniature topiary, and the costume of those who walk, make love, play music or dance in it. An illumination from a late-fifteenth-century Flemish manuscript of the 'Roman de la Rose' shows an elegant young man seeking admittance to this jardin d'amour within which another young man can be seen playing a stringed instrument. But there is nothing about the clothing of either of them which would relate them to the garden.

For such a connexion we have to move on a couple of centuries to the Versailles of Louis XIV where there is a recognisable link between garden design and clothes. By then France set fashion in the arts. Indeed fashion, commodity design, taste and textile manufacture were linked into the political rhetoric of the French garden. By then fashion as we know it in clothes today had emerged. That had only begun in the fourteenth century when the mercantile classes with their new-found wealth began to ape the dress of their aristocratic betters who, in turn, devised new fashions and even legislation which would set their own clothes apart. But it was Louis XIV and his great minister Colbert who realised the economic and political potential of fashion. Colbert's policy was to promote luxury goods, above all rich silks and lace of French manufacture, making it mandatory for the aristocracy to wear them, thus simultaneously promoting French industry and fashion.

It was the French garden tradition which developed the 'parterre de broderie', a form of gardening which drew on textile and lace patterns.

In both Italy and France, which together had set garden style for two centuries, the fashion for floral designs in clothing textiles became attractive

1

1 *Joseph Wright of Derby,*
Brooke Boothby, *1781*

2 *The most elegant couple:*
Sir Harold Nicholson and Vita
Sackville-West in their garden
at Sissinghurst

3 *Claude Monet in a summer*
suit at Giverny, 1900

4 Habit de Jardinier, *a*
seventeenth-century engraving
by the Bonnart family

5 *'Strange instrument picture'*
from Nathaniel Lloyd's 'Garden
Craftsmanship in Yew and
Box', 1929

2

3

Habit de Jardinier.

4

5

to the elites. **The French silk industry specialised in light silks with elegant and refined designs directly echoing the patterns seen in the parterres de broderie.** When parterre design went in the direction of strings of laurels and garlands of flowers men's coats and waistcoats introduced borders of flowers and leaf patterns.

In this way there was a visual continuity between what the nobility wore as they paraded in the garden and what the landscape created by the great designer André Le Nôtre had imposed on its surface at Versailles.

By the 1680s that had become a showplace of French style, copied throughout the courts of Europe. **All of this, however, was to be swept away with the arrival of 'le jardin anglais' which emerged in its various**

**guises in England during the
opening decades of the
eighteenth century.** That was
a style which in its various phases was
to slowly sweep through Europe as far
as the Russia of Catherine the Great and
also to reach America.
Can we adumbrate a similar symbiosis
between the new garden style and
the revolution in men's fashion which
stemmed from England again during
exactly the same period? I believe
that we can.

Horace Walpole was to sum up the new
style in his observation about one of
its pioneers, William Kent: "He leaped
the fence, and saw that all nature was a
garden."
**Gradually the symmetry, the
ordered clipped topiary and
the elaborate parterres were
banished. Gardens ceased**

to be about pattern of a kind which could be reflected in textiles worn on the person but became a series of deliberately composed pictures through which the owner and his guests strolled. They could, of course, be dotted with temples, obelisks, urns and gazebos in commemoration of this or that heroic person to stir the mind and the emotions. Such domains called for a very different kind of dress, one attuned with the world of nature. As early as the 1740s a few continental aristocrats and wealthy merchants began to adopt the dress of the English upper classes.

By the second half of the century Anglo-mania had swept through France and Europe and English style was to dominate men's clothing until the second half of the twentieth century.

That style is summed up in English portraits of the period where the preference is for placing a sitter in the open air in what the viewer would take to be part of the landscaped parkland of their country estate. Except for the grandest occasions embroidery, rich patterned fabrics and lace were out replaced by plain fabrics, spotless linen and muslin.

This English sartorial statement was associated by visitors from abroad with a country which had a parliamentary democracy as against their monarchical absolutism. The English aristocracy prided themselves less on their attendance at court than presiding over their landed estates which they landscaped in the latest fashion by the likes of 'Capability' Brown with clumps of trees, winding pathways and serpentine lakes, all viewed as somehow reflecting English freedoms and liberties.

**The ideal attire for the
English gentleman was simple
country clothes or those for
the hunt or the shoot. They of
course embodied a new form
of sartorial elegance, seen
as attuned with the world of
nature rediscovered, in which
to stroll through these vast
gardens.**

Joseph Wright of Derby's portrait of
Brooke Boothby dated 1781 is the
epitome of this new style of dress. We see
him reclining in a wood by a babbling
brook, a setting which would be read
by the viewer as part of his estate at
Ashbourne Hall, Derbyshire.
**The muted browns of his attire
speak eloquently of the new
simplicity, a double-breasted
frock-coat, a very short
double-breasted waistcoat, an**

**unadorned broad-brimmed hat
and a cravat of plain muslin.
The unbuttoned coat and
waistcoat add an element
of sophisticated deshabille.
The contrast with the highly
patterned and embroidered
dress of the French court
could not be more striking.**
Similarly, four years later we catch
that same simplicity in one of Thomas
Gainsborough's most famous pictures,
The Morning Walk. The young William
Hallett walks arm in arm with his recent
bride through the grounds of his house.
Again the fabrics are plain, this time blue
with gold buttons and there is the same
plain muslin stock. How can I draw this
little history of the relationship of men's
fashion to the garden to a close?
**All garden clothes for men
descend from the English
stylistic revolution of the**

eighteenth century which was to produce in the nineteenth trousers and then the suit. They are and remain country clothes. All the great gardeners I have known, such as Sir Geoffrey Jellicoe, Russell Page and Lanning Roper, have worn country tweeds, either an entire tweed suit or a tweed jacket with corduroy or twill trousers. To this would be added a woollen shirt, often checked, a tie and maybe a waistcoat or pullover. The shoes would be heavy and sensible. They often stayed dressed like that even in summer and certainly, brought up within the restrained etiquette of correct dress, they would never shed a jacket. And jeans, typical of our own age, would have been regarded as beyond the pale.

But all three men belonged to the
first three quarters of the last century.
In the main, I recall, they always
appeared crumpled and the clothes
ancient, worn as badges of past labour
but also of love and association.
So many clothes worn in the garden
are hung in a lobby by what is known
as the garden entrance of a house.
There would be piled-up Wellington
boots, rubber overshoes, walking
sticks and umbrellas, various country
rain proofs and a festoon of hats
for both winter and summer.
Sometimes venturing into the garden
can resemble dipping into the dressing-
up box. In an old country house some of
the items would have been worn by the
present owner's father or grandfather.

We can perhaps explore this with
a few images. One of the most famous
late-nineteenth-century gardens is that

created by the Impressionist painter
Claude Monet at Giverny. There are
countless photographs of the artist in
his garden and almost without exception
they record him in a crumpled tweed
suit, the trousers held up by braces.
He wears a shirt, sturdy shoes and a felt
hat on his head. In summer the suit
is made of a lighter fabric and he sports
a straw hat.
Harold Nicholson and Vita Sackville-West
are two other garden icons, creators
of Sissinghurst in Kent, one of the most
influential gardens of the twentieth
century. Here again we encounter the
same felt hat, an old tweed jacket,
pullover and baggy trousers. It is Vita
who adds a touch of masculine style with
her knee breeches and boots into the
top of which she tucked her secateurs.
Lanning Roper, who worked on both
sides of the Atlantic, in his portrait by
Snowdon purveys the same garden image:

check shirt, tie, tweed jacket, pocket handkerchief, corduroy trousers and Wellington boots.

All these images exude practicality, an expectancy of bad weather, of having to step into mud or clamber up somewhere, of being assailed by the prickly branch of a rambling rose. **But, you may well ask, don't gardening folk ever dress up? Well, yes, they do, but only for horticultural shows, above all for that mecca of the gardening world, the opening day of the Chelsea Flower Show on the third Monday in May. Such shows betoken summer and then it is often out with the patterned waistcoat, the blazer and the straw hat. These are the only times when I see garden**

**owners, designers, nurserymen
and hands-on gardeners dress
up, even if it is only with
a floral buttonhole.**

François Berthoud
*Born in Switzerland,
1961, lives and works in
Zurich. He is known for
his fashion illustrations.
Since the mid-1980s,
François Berthoud has
been mainly engaged
in artistic activities.
His high-impact images
bring art, fashion
and communication
together. He has
published books, staged
exhibitions and realized
special fashion projects.
He is a contributor
to major magazines
worldwide.*

Sir Roy Strong
*is a writer and
historian and
gardener. He was
Director of the
National Portrait
Gallery (1967–73)
and of the Victoria
and Albert Museum
(1974–87). In his
capacity as a
gardener he has
helped the Prince
of Wales, the late
Gianni Versace and
Sir Elton John with
their gardens. He is
the author of many
books on garden
design and history.*

*The publisher would like to thank the following
for the use of their photographs in this publication,
pp. 14–15:
1. Tate Gallery, London
2. Courtesy of the Cecil Beaton Studio Archive
at Sotheby's, London
3. Private Collection, Paris / Bridgeman Art Library
4. Musée de la Ville de Paris, Musée Carnavalet, Paris
/ Lauros / Giraudon / Bridgeman Art Library
5. From Nathaniel Lloyd's 'Garden Craftsmanship in
Yew and Box,' 1929, Courtesy of Great Dixter, Kent*

Picture research by Lynda Marshall

**cover and back cover image
by François Berthoud**